CRYSTAL WRITES

STORY OF A 12 - YEAR - OLD GIRL. HOW SHE WRITES, PLANS, AND FLOPS. DAYS IN HER LIFE. ETC.

FAHIMA

I'm a 12-year-old girl. I have always wanted to be a writer. One day I will publish my stories all over the world. with lots of love and happiness, I present every story.

Contents

CHAPTER ONE

Here It starts...

She Goes and lies on her bed sadly with disappointment. Her name is Crystal. She wants to be a writer. Not later Just right now. before she becomes a teen she wants to become a writer. Hi, I'm 12 years old girl. I want to be a writer but I think nobody should judge me; She's a Teen so She got the maturity to be a writer. That's wrong anyone can be a writer. I've read a little about a writer. She's Abhijita Gupta Youngest writer in the world. She became a writer at the age of Seven. I have always admired her. My Brother, Mother, and Friends are my only Motivation to write stories. My Brother; is an Awesome writer and my role - model, He is 17 years older than me. My mom; always tells me I'm a good writer. One day all will love my stories. My friends; always Love my stories and force me to fulfill the story. And also, they demotivate me. My mom; Your writing is good but nobody will love it in our family. they will not like what you do now and you're a Muslim if someone knows you want to become a writer then they will start telling you advice. My brother; You wasting your time. I started writing even younger than you and I posted in lots of Magazines that nothing was helpful. You just study that's enough. Friends; just ignore me. Cause I'm a weirdo a little more mature. I know lots of things. I just thought If I gained knowledge I can create better stories. But that didn't create better stories. It just created my friends to ignore me. Most of the time I was left out. But still, my friends didn't bully me at all. Even though they discourage me They never let me down totally.

CHAPTER TWO

Friendship

Katherine is my best friend. One day in our class, our English teacher told us to act in a play. I'm the team leader. and Katherine was also a part of the play. Her acting skills were awesome. Her English sounded a little more formal but her acting skills were awesome. The reason why I didn't tell you about my father is, He just hated my brother just because he want to be a writer. I never opened up about my writing just because I don't want anyone to hate me. The wonderful thing that happened in my life is my pets. I had a total of Five cockatiels and One Alexandrine Parrot. They're not just birds, They're my friends and also an important part of my family. Two of my cockatiel died and my Only Parrot died. I'm really sad for them. I can never think about their death. They are still living in my life...

Family and routine

My father doesn't have any interest in birds. But I live with them. I Love my pets than my family. Every day of my life is interesting. I wake up and see the clock, it's 10:32 In the morning. I again fell asleep. at last at 11:45 I decided to wake up. Just brushed, washed my face, and ate my Breakfast which was made in the morning at 8:00. After finishing breakfast I just go lie in my bed open my laptop watch Netflix, and Sitcoms. At least for two hours, I do nothing. Then Afternoon Lunch comes, My Mom calls me more than 47 times I keep on telling her 2 minutes, please. Then my mm loses her patience and starts scolding me finally I go and eat lunch. After lunch, I'll Watch my Laptop I'll check emails from my friends and I'll be chatting with them. Then I'll go to the mosque. I'll Come at 6:15 in the evening. I drink my tea. Then I'll start doing my homework. Mostly I like to do the homework in the evening after 6:00. I'll finish everything within 9:00 and I will be typing my stories or What happened in my today. That's the fun part ever.

CHAPTER FOUR

My dream

My dream is to publish at least one book before the age of 13.

I can write stories but I don't know where to publish them. I lose hope sometimes. But when the new day starts, New motivations cross my mind. I love writing and really obsessed with it. How will you feel If you love to do something but you can't do it right? I've faced it lots of times. I love to dance but I can't dance properly. I've been selected for lots of dance events in my school but Within 3 days they get Annoyed with me I can never coordinate with my dance mates. I Love editing in photoshop and I love playing games.

I like to be aesthetic but I'm not much organized. I love Bullet Journals. But they are way too expensive. I make Diy Journals I always try to maintain it but I cannot. I write a diary where I express my emotions and feelings That's the only place where I complain I share everything. But my fear is nobody should read it. But they won't listen to me. Wantedly they want to read it and tease me.

CHAPTER FIVE

First story

My first story was in the Horror genre. I only knew to write horror stories but now I learned a few more like fantasies and Magic stories. I usually write stories after getting inspiration but today I didn't get any inspiration just because it's my story. I started writing stories before 2 - 3 years. When I studied in my 4th grade and was 9 years old I wrote a very long story for the first time. then When I studied in 5th grade and I was 10 years old I started getting compliments. I was really happy about this. But soon they started ignoring me. Still, they love my stories...

CHAPTER SIX

The interesting part and a short story

There are two interesting parts of my life and they are my Parrots and My only brother. My Brother is really really supportive. The age difference between me and my brother is 17 years. Now I'm 12 years old and he is twenty-nine years old. He is a caring, protective, smart lovable brother. Let me tell you a short Christmas story. There were two people in opposite homes one was rich, Stephen and the other was poor Christopher. they both love to worship and pray a lot. they are so religious. One day they both had the same dream. In that dream, a bright light talked with them and told them; I'm the light fairy. I'm the queen of happy miracles. If you use this opportunity and won the test you will always stay rich and wealthy. The next day Christopher met Stephen and told everything about the dream and Stephen told him he had the same dream too. Today is Christmas night so, the test will be conducted today at midnight, Right? asked Christopher. Yes, Told Stephen. Soon the clock's time turns 12'O clock. Christopher and Stephen Vanished from their home and appeared in a dark room. They both had Two sacks of gold in front of them. and two statues of god on the side.

CHAPTER SEVEN

Short story ends..

Now they hear the same voice which was heard in the dream. It told; Who runs ten times around this place and also spends 2 minutes to worship god win. Note: don't waste even 1 minute on either of them. Let's start. Christopher and Stephen got 12 minutes for this test. Christopher used his first 2 minutes to pray. and used one minute for each round. Stephen ran very fast and he worshiped after every two rounds. when the time ran out, Christopher exactly ran 10 rounds and also did his prayer at the starting. But Stephen only ran 5 rounds and prayed 5 times. Stephen thought he is the winner because he was worshiping a lot than Christopher but the light fairy appeared in front of them and told Christopher is the winner. Christopher got happy. But Stephen got angry and yelled at the light fairy. The light fairy told with a happy smile on her face; Christopher followed the rules and used his opportunity but you did not do it you wasted time on worshiping gods. It's very good to worship gods but you also have to do something don't always be dependent, God cannot always be with you so only he gave you a brain to do what you decide to do. Stephen remained rich but, Christopher became a millionaire.

My Lifetime Passion...

Hope you liked my story and my life story. My dream is to become a writer not afterward just right now before I become 13. I told this, my mom told me You're not going to become a writer just because you're already a writer. these are both reasons why I still write, the other reason is that my brother is a writer so he always inspires me with his creativity it's my time to show my own creativity.

Positivity!

All people discourage you when you have the courage to write so please Ignore negativity and
discouragements.

The End...

You should not leave your writing just here.
    Continue... continue... continue
    Till heaven!!!
    ~Thank You

Fahima